Polesden Lacey

SURREY

A souvenir guide

National Trust

A VILLA WITH A VIEW

The high downland setting of the magnificent house provides panoramic views south across the deep valley to Ranmore Woods and Common on the southern skyline, and Box Hill to the east. The surrounding 940 acres (380 hectares) of farmland and woodland were cultivated to support the life and finances of successive owners, who added to the gardens and landscape.

An ancient estate

25 miles from central London, Polesden Lacey is a remarkable survival of a small, self-contained agricultural estate which has remained largely intact since the Middle Ages.

A substantial house was built on the present site around 1630 to replace a medieval farmhouse. From 1797 to 1816 it was home to the politician and playwright Richard Brinsley Sheridan, who described it as 'the nicest place, within a prudent distance of town, in England.'

'A peep of beautiful distance.'

Joseph Farington, 1803

In 1818 it was sold to Joseph Bonsor, who commissioned Thomas Cubitt to design and build a new house on the site, which forms the core of the present building. In 1853 Polesden Lacey was sold to Sir Walter Farquhar, who extended the Walled Garden and formalised the planting. In 1902 the estate was acquired by Sir Clinton Dawkins, who employed the architect Ambrose Poynter to make major alterations to the house.

A status symbol for the new rich

The agricultural depression of the late 19th century made running a country estate as a business very hard, but the consequent drop in land prices made the acquisition of a country house both affordable and desirable for the newly rich, who had benefited from the expansion of the British Empire and its vast trading operations. For those who could afford it, a 'country seat' was an eminently desirable status symbol.

In 1906 Polesden Lacey was bought by the Hon. Mr and Mrs Ronald Greville, wealthy and well-connected friends of Edward VII. He was the eldest son and heir of 2nd Lord Greville, and his wife Margaret was the sole heiress to an

Mrs Greville

Polesden Lacey was the country home of the dynamic and ambitious Margaret Greville. She rose from obscure origins to attain political influence, great wealth and the friendship of royalty. An inveterate traveller and relentless celebrity-hunter, she could be both discreetly charitable and personally waspish. She bequeathed Polesden Lacey and most of her other property to the National Trust in 1942, in memory of her father – one of the first such bequests of a country house, its estate and its collections to the charity.

The natural daughter of William McEwan, a millionaire Scottish brewer and philanthropist, she declared, 'I'd rather be a beeress than a peeress.' Mrs Greville's immense fortune allowed her to maintain her position as one of the most influential hostesses in Europe for nearly four decades. Princes and maharajahs, viceroys and prime ministers, ambassadors and captains of industry enjoyed her lavish hospitality, but there was a price: she often aroused strong and contradictory reactions. The diarist Chips Channon wrote that there was 'no-one on earth so skilfully malicious as old Maggie'. But when she died, the Queen Mother wrote wistfully to Osbert Sitwell, 'I shall miss her very much.'

Under the watchful eye of its demanding chatelaine, Polesden Lacey became the perfect setting for pleasure and leisure, for gossip, luxury and discreet dalliance among the upper classes. 'I never follow people into their bedrooms', remarked Mrs Greville.

Right Mrs Greville, painted by Carolus-Duran at the time of her marriage in 1891
Below An Italian Renaissance maiolica plate from Mrs Greville's superb collection
Opposite Polesden Lacey enjoys magnificent views over the valley to the south

immense brewing fortune. They commissioned the architectural firm of Mewès and Davis, fresh from their triumph in designing the Ritz Hotel in London, to make further changes. Money was no object, and the interior decorating firm of White, Allom & Co. used architectural salvage and sumptuous fittings to create an impressive, luxurious country house fit for royalty and reminiscent of the best type of Edwardian hotel.

Mrs Greville was also keen to combine her expanding collection of old master paintings, fine furniture and *objets d'art* with 'state-of-the-art' technology. *En suite* bathrooms were installed, bedrooms had telephones, the food was exquisite, and the grounds were designed to entertain, with a golf course, croquet lawn and game-bird shooting.

TOUR OF THE HOUSE

THE CENTRAL HALL

The Central Hall was designed by Ambrose Poynter as an informal sitting room, with groups of sofas and chairs, rather than as a mere lobby. It was where Mrs Greville's guests were welcomed on arrival, and it was provided with discreet but useful facilities – a cloakroom, wardrobes and a lavatory. Every evening, at 6pm, the footman would lay out drinks on the 17th-century refectory table, while the gramophone would play the latest hits by Noel Coward. When she was sure that all her guests were gathered attentively below, Mrs Greville would descend the staircase slowly, pausing at the landing for maximum impact before completing her entrée among her visitors.

Below The Central Hall

Furnishings
The décor for the Central Hall was designed by Mrs Greville's decorators, White, Allom & Co. They introduced the massive silver-plated 17th-century-French-style chandelier (actually a late Victorian copy) and the silver-plated sconces. Magnificent Flemish tapestries, dating from the 16th, 17th and early 18th centuries, complement the French walnut sofa and six armchairs with their 19th-century *gros-point* upholstery.

Woodwork
Along the fireplace wall is an intricately carved reredos (screen behind the altar), originally installed in St Matthew's, one of Christopher Wren's City churches. All the woodwork for St Matthew's was carved by Edward Pierce (*c.*1630–95), in a style associated with Grinling

Gibbons. In 1883 the church was demolished and its furnishings were auctioned. White, Allom & Co. acquired the reredos at a later date and installed it at Polesden Lacey, where it was modified to fit the space. Set off by a marble chimneypiece in 17th-century style, the blazing fire was a welcome sight for Mrs Greville's guests as they arrived for the weekend.

THE STAIRCASE

The staircase sweeps up to the first-floor gallery, and it was from this ideal vantage point that Mrs Greville and her elderly father would watch her servants and their families enjoying the musical parties she held for them annually in the Central Hall.

Ceramics

Mrs Greville was an ardent collector of Renaissance-era maiolica (Italian tin-glazed earthenware). Lustrous in colour and bold in design, maiolica was created for display as well as practical use. Mrs Greville gradually acquired a collection of museum-quality pieces, and paid as much as £483 for a single rarity, a huge sum in the 1920s. She had a special cabinet built on the staircase to house her favourite treasures.

Above A silver-plated 17th-century-French-style ceiling light

'One uses up so many red carpets in a season ....'

Margaret Greville

Left *The Judgement of Paris*; maiolica plate, produced at Castel Durante, near Urbino, in 1524-6

THE DINING ROOM

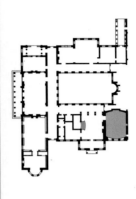

The Dining Room was designed in the French Neo-classical style, with elliptical ends and crimson silk damask wallcoverings. The pelmets are from the Regency era. The oval table currently on display has been arranged to seat eight, for more intimate dinners. The room could be transformed by bringing in a bigger table, to seat 20. The Dining Room was also used for refreshments at the annual Servants' Ball.

Pictures
Mrs Greville chose to display her most impressive British portrait paintings in this room: there are important works by Raeburn, Lely, Lawrence and Reynolds. Her favourite painting was the Benjamin Constant portrait of Mr McEwan, painted in 1900, which was described by Margaret Greville as a 'striking likeness', though her father never liked the painting. Mrs Greville would preside over dinner seated at the head of the table, with her beloved father looking over her shoulder.

A drunken butler

Glorious as the setting was, Mrs Greville's staff would occasionally let her down. On one occasion, it was apparent that the butler was intoxicated. She wrote a surreptitious note saying, 'You are drunk; leave the room at once', summoned the butler and placed it on his salver. He bowed courteously, advanced to the guest of honour, Sir Austen Chamberlain, and presented the note to him. The eminent politician spent the rest of the meal in mystified silence. When she explained the misunderstanding, he replied that it was the first time he had ever been silenced by a drunken butler.

Superfluous silver

The table would be laid with specially-made Irish linen tablecloths –
each one took a year to weave – and individual settings of magnificent
silver for every guest. Mrs Greville was a serious collector of early
English silver, and some of her tankards and a Charles II *tazza* (salver)
are on display on the table. Winston Churchill once famously
complained that the ornate silverware was impeding his view of his
fellow guests. Mrs Greville ordered everything superfluous cleared away
from the table and acidly asked him, 'Is that better for you?'

Polesden Lacey

The fish is good, the meat is fine,
No need to praise the luscious wine!
The beds and linen 'beat the band',
The water's hot, the butler's grand.

There's golf & tennis and every game,
What other comfort can I name?
But why speak of wine & meat?
'Tis our hostess whose [sic] so sweet.

Lord Plunket

Above The Dining Room
was designed by Ambrose
Poynter in 1903–5. The late
18th-century white marble
chimneypiece was
introduced by Mrs Greville

Food for the famous

The Dining Room was designed to be
highly efficient – to the right of the
fireplace is a jib door, leading to the
Serving Room, Kitchen and other
offices. Such attention to detail ensured
that the food arrived piping hot, while
the champagne remained chilled, a
welcome novelty compared with many
country house dinners. Typically, a ten-
course meal would be served, with
excellent wines, though the portions
were much smaller than would be
normal today.

Mrs Greville was renowned for her
excellent French cuisine, which was
described in the *Daily Telegraph* in 1930
as 'unsurpassed anywhere'. She often
employed female chefs, which was
unusual for the time, and was proud of
using produce from the estate.

THE PICTURE CORRIDOR

The Picture Corridor makes up three sides of the central courtyard, and acted both as the main route to the formal rooms on the ground floor, and as Mrs Greville's picture gallery. Her best paintings were originally hung at her London house, but on her death her collections were amalgamated and rehung at Polesden Lacey. She was a shrewd and committed collector, advised by experts such as Agnew's and Dr Tancred Borenius.

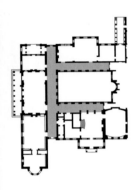

The Jacobean oak *panelling* was adapted to fit, and the barrel-vaulted plaster *ceiling* was copied from the magnificent early 17th-century ceiling in the Long Gallery at Chastleton in Oxfordshire.

The antique Roman *sarcophagus* dates from 3AD, and although it has lost its dedication, the carvings of elephants and giraffes imply that its original occupant had an African background. In Mrs Greville's day, the sarcophagus was topped by an oak lid and would support dramatic flower arrangements.

Left Chinese export porcelain soup-tureen in the form of a goose, *c.*1780

Below *The Virgin and Child enthroned with Saints* is an early 14th-century triptych of Italo-Byzantine origin. The gabled peaks contain depictions of the Annunciation, flanking a scene of the Crucifixion. Below is the central image of the Madonna and Child, and the saints include Francis, Dominic and St Louis of Toulouse. Portable altarpieces of this type were votive objects of great intricacy and desirability in pre-Renaissance Italy

OPPOSITE

Left The Picture Corridor runs around three sides of the central courtyard

Right *An Officer Making His Bow to a Lady*, by Gerard Ter Borch. Painted about 1662, this ambiguous scene represents an illicit assignation between a young lady and an officer. Intriguingly, the woman is believed to be the artist's own half-sister, Gesina

THE LIBRARY

The Library was designed in the French style for Mrs Greville by Mewès and Davis, and features their trademark mirror-backed doors. This was one of her favourite rooms; the warm glowing colours are offset by some excellent blue and white Chinese Kangxi porcelain (1662–1722) and Japanese Imari ware. The comfortable furniture is a blend of English, French and Italian dating from the 17th and 18th centuries, largely re-upholstered with contemporary needlework in the Edwardian era.

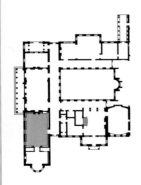

Books
The books were acquired for the convenience and amusement of Mrs Greville's guests, to complement her excellent cuisine and general level of luxury. The room evokes the library of an exclusive gentlemen's club rather than the more idiosyncratic collection of a single individual. Some of the books now here once belonged to the staff library in the stable courtyard.

Photographs
Facing the fireplace is an early 19th-century mahogany *writing table*. This was the cockpit from which Mrs Greville steered much of her social life. The desktop is covered with her favourite framed photographs: Mr and Mrs McEwan, the Aga Khan, Ronald Greville, George VI, Queen Elizabeth and the two princesses.

Below The tortoiseshell, ivory and ebony inlaid walnut coffer on a stand, c.1600, was given to Mrs Greville in 1920 by her close friend Princess Victoria Eugénie, who married Alfonso XIII of Spain in 1906

Above Housed in two cases on the central table is an important collection of miniature paintings, mostly acquired between 1891 and 1910. The miniatures date from the 17th to the early 19th century. Mrs Greville was fascinated by portraits in all media – she prided herself on being a shrewd judge of character

'My dear, I know I am not an educated woman.'

Margaret Greville

Above The Library was designed for Mrs Greville by Mewès and Davis. The large early 19th-century mahogany writing table is covered with numerous framed photographs of Mrs Greville's guests

Right Above the 18th-century fireplace hangs the *Portrait of a Boy with a Sheep*, by Aelbert Cuyp (1620-91). The gold medal and chain were worn by boys at this era, although children of both sexes wore skirts. This is a rare early portrait by this artist, who was only nineteen when he executed it

THE STUDY

The adjacent Study and adjoining cloakroom were created by Mewès and Davis to make a 'private sanctum' for Mrs Greville. It was in this room that she spent much of the day towards the end of her life, when mobility problems and recurrent bronchitis confined her to a wheelchair.

'She sat back in a large chair, like a Phoenician goddess, while the cabinet minister or ambassador leant forward attentively. I have no doubt that she had considerable influence.' **Kenneth Clark**

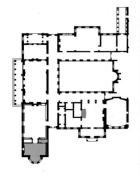

The panorama looking south across the valley is spectacular, so the architects devised an ingenious solution: they ran the flue from the fireplace to one side so as not to impede the view. In the evenings, servants would pull sliding mirrors across the windows, creating a snug and intimate room, ideal for the exchange of confidences.

There were originally 'two stuffed armchairs' in the Study, and it was here that Mrs Greville would interview her guest of honour immediately after dinner, while the other guests amused themselves in the Saloon.

Ceramics

The glazed showcase of 18th-century Meissen and Furstenberg porcelain includes a rare *tea and coffee service*, *c*.1770, decorated with *singeries* (monkeys pursuing human activities). Though an avid and discriminating collector, Mrs Greville would occasionally feed her beloved pet dogs from one of her Meissen bowls as a special treat.

Friends remembered

Some of her closest friends are remembered in this room: there is an 18th-century Indian *chess set* given by Queen Mary, and a pair of Japanese black and gold lacquer *tea canisters*, given as a Christmas present to Mrs Greville by the Queen in 1919. A formal *portrait photograph* of Queen Ena of Spain belies the closeness of their friendship. Mrs Greville famously invited her other friends to a 'wee, wee party' she was giving in London for Queen Ena, and was to leave a substantial sum to the deposed monarch in her will.

Opposite The Study was designed by Mewès and Davis as a private room for Mrs Greville. The mahogany writing desk in the bow window is English *c*.1800. Mirrored window shutters open to reveal the view south across the valley

13

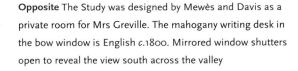

Left The Duke and Duchess of York (later George VI and Queen Elizabeth) spent part of their honeymoon at Polesden Lacey in 1923

THE SALOON

Mrs Greville's architects and decorators installed a sumptuous carved and panelled *salone* from an Italian palace of the early 18th century. The gilded panelling is offset with crimson brocade, and the floors are of herringbone parquet covered in Persian carpets.

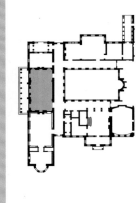

The French-influenced Italianate theme continues in the painted canvases let into the ceiling, with rectangular panels depicting *putti* holding garlands of flowers, combined with scenes from the Old Testament. The furniture is of the highest quality and largely French, Louis XV or XVI. Japanese lacquer cabinets and a Steinway boudoir grand piano complete the air of opulence.

Favourite objects

This room was the grandest in the house and designed to impress. Here Mrs Greville displayed some of her favourite *objets d'art*, including Meissen and Sèvres porcelain and Chinese and Japanese ceramics. In showcases and cabinets are smaller, more intricate objects, such as Chinese vases, bowls, snuff bottles and figures. She was particularly fond of small-scale Fabergé or Cartier carvings of animals, which were highly collectable among the smart circles of Edwardian society. Mrs Greville would often draw attention to these and say pointedly to her house guests, 'Lord so-and-so bought me this to say thank you' – a less-than-subtle hint that she would welcome further trophies.

Among her prize possessions were an oval tortoiseshell *snuffbox* with Edward VII's cipher on the lid, and two *brooches*, given to Mrs Greville in 1909 as a memento of his stay at Polesden Lacey.

The *portrait of Mrs Greville* was painted in 1889, when she was an unmarried 26-year-old, by Herman Schmiechen, a painter of Society portraits. The subject seems almost demure and hesitant; it contrasts greatly with the vibrant Carolus-Duran painting in the Picture Corridor (see p.3).

Above Two miniature Fabergé dogs

Right Mrs Greville's collection of pill boxes

The Saloon was the focus of social life for Mrs Greville's weekend house-parties during Ascot Week and at Christmas. Tea would be served here for larger parties, and guests were encouraged to mingle and enjoy themselves, either around the piano, or by watching the antics of professional comedians and music hall stars engaged by Mrs Greville for after-dinner performances. Confidences were exchanged, secrets traded and pressing political and diplomatic issues explored in this ornate setting.

'I want a room fit to entertain Maharajahs in.' Mrs Greville's instruction to her architect

Above The Saloon is extravagantly carved and panelled, using early 18th-century panelling from an Italian *palazzo*. Red brocade (replaced in 2003) is let into the panelling

THE TEA ROOM

French in style and intimate in atmosphere, the Tea Room occupies the south-west corner of the house and so is ideally placed to catch the sun each afternoon. It was designed by Mewès and Davis in 1906–9 to take advantage of the magnificent views over the South Vista and the Rose Garden, with French windows, in the restrained style of Louis XVI, c.1785.

Pictures and furniture

The panelling surrounds a series of late 18th-century pastoral landscapes in the style of Fragonard or Boucher, but they are probably Flemish or Dutch in origin. Much of the fine rococo furniture now in this room is from Mrs Greville's London home, 16 Charles Street, and includes a pair of small giltwood sofas covered in tapestry, dating from around 1780, which are known as *confidents* or *tête à têtes*, because their small size invited intimate conversations.

Silver

The early English silver on display here is a small fraction of Mrs Greville's excellent collection, an interest she inherited from her father. The silver **teapot** on a stand to the right of the far window is by Marshall & Sons, and engraved with Mr McEwan's initials. The **salver** on a trumpet foot is by Samuel Hood, London, and is dated 1698; the **cake basket** in the form of a scallop shell is by Phillips Garden, London, 1750. The silver **teapots** are English, early 18th-century; the smaller round one is probably by John Fawdery, London, 1729; the larger is by Gabriel Sleath, London, 1717.

Red carpet treatment

Up to 20 people could take tea in this room, and it was a popular haunt of Queen Mary, who would often telephone to announce herself for tea that afternoon. On one such occasion, Mrs Greville, aware that her famous red carpets were wearing thin in places, hurried to London and back, returning with 20 antelope skins to cover the threadbare patches.

Tea

Beverley Nichols vividly remembered tea times at Polesden Lacey:

'Tea is at 5 o'clock ... and not at 5 minutes past ... which means the Spanish Ambassador, who has gone for a walk down the yew avenue, hastily retraces his steps, and the Chancellor of the Exchequer ... hurries down the great staircase, and that the various gentlemen rise from their chaise-longues ... and join the procession to the tea-room. The tea-pots, cream-jugs, the milk-pits and the sugar basins are of Queen Anne silver; the tea service is Meissen; and the doilies, heavily monogrammed, are of Chantilly lace.'

'Maggie's teas were terrific, with great Georgian teapots and Indian or China, and muffins and cream cakes and silver kettles sending up their steam, and Queen Mary saying "Indian, if you please, and no sugar..."'

Mrs Greville's cuisine was justifiably famous, and she usually employed a female cook. Among these was Mrs Isabella Menzies, who was famed for her Wemyss Rich Chocolate Cake.

Above The Tea-Room: 'Displaying some of the smaller items of French furniture from her London house and it now has the appearance of a small drawing room or boudoir...'

Opposite The Rococo pastoral scenes were inspired by 18th-century French artists such as François Boucher, but are most likely to be Flemish or Dutch

THE BILLIARD ROOM

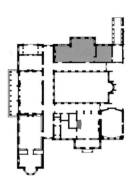

The Billiard Room, and the adjacent Smoking Room and Gun Room, comprise a bastion of masculinity, redolent of the Bachelor's Wing in earlier houses. The Billiard Room was created by Ambrose Poynter in 1903–5, and only altered cosmetically in Mrs Greville's time. It has recently been restored to the way it looked between 1908 and 1941.

A self-made man

The room is dominated by an evocative portrait of William McEwan, painted in 1901 by W.W. Ouless. The enigmatic Mr McEwan made a fortune in brewing, had a successful career as an MP for Central Edinburgh, and quietly married Mrs Greville's widowed mother, Helen Anderson, in 1885. Despite his philanthropy, Scottish society believed (with some justification) that he was the natural father of Margaret, and was scandalised. On his death in 1913, she inherited his entire estate, and found herself one of the wealthiest women in Britain.

A gentleman's club in miniature, the room has two main focuses: the area around the fireplace, with books, easy chairs and writing tables; and the larger section, dominated by a mahogany-framed billiard-table by Burroughs and Watts, with a sofa and armchairs for spectators. Photographs of military men and their memorabilia abound; the young Prince Albert (later George VI), the Duke of Cambridge, and Arthur Paget.

This room provided a bolthole from the necessary demands of polite society, and a venue for men to talk business, politics and sport. They played cards, listened to the radio and exchanged fruity stories. Needless to say, it was a favourite after-dinner haunt of King Edward VII.

THE SMOKING ROOM

Providing a smoking room was the duty of every self-respecting Edwardian hostess. Gentlemen needed somewhere to retire to smoke after dinner, as it was considered risqué to smoke in front of ladies, until the practice was endorsed by Edward VII.

The Smoking Room at Polesden Lacey is now laid out as a museum, with family photographs and memorabilia of High Society vying for wall space. Among those featured are Lord and Lady Louis Mountbatten, with the future Edward VIII; Mrs Keppel with her daughter, Violet; Lord Reading, Viceroy of India; and the lavishly dressed Maharajah of Cooch Behar.

The Polesden Lacey *visitors' book* was originally in the Entrance Hall, and the first signatory was Edward VII, in 1907. Two 'Dinner Books', one from Charles Street and the other from Polesden, list all Mrs Greville's lunch, dinner and weekend guests from 1926 till 1940, and in many cases give details of the menu. There are testimonial albums on the lives and careers of Mr McEwan and Ronald Greville, and the handwritten notes kept by both Margaret Greville and her father, recording their art acquisitions and their thoughts about their collections. There are also the cufflinks given to Mrs Greville's major domo and right-hand man, Mr Bole the House Steward. The cufflinks were a royal memento, following the Duke and Duchess of York's honeymoon at Polesden in 1923. The cufflinks are on permanent loan from the Bole family, and bear the initial 'A' for Albert – the family name by which the future King George VI was known.

Ronald Greville

The other important man in Mrs Greville's life is also remembered here: her husband, the Hon. Ronald Henry Fulke Greville (1864–1908). Eldest son of the 2nd Lord Greville, he became a Captain in the 1st Life Guards, and later Conservative MP for Bradford. A member of the racy Marlborough House set, the circumstances of his meeting and engagement to Margaret remain mysterious, but their wedding in 1891 lead to a genuinely happy marriage, the only regret being their inability to have children. In 1908, 'Ronnie' was diagnosed with throat cancer, and died of pneumonia following an emergency operation. Described as 'witty, good-natured, typically Irish', he was sincerely mourned by his widow.

THE GARDEN

There are historic references to 'the garden at Polesdene' as early as 1333, but most records of the estate start in the 18th century. Polesden Lacey is now the fourth most-visited property in the care of the National Trust, with about 300,000 people visiting a year. Caring for the land while encouraging access is a challenge for the charity.

This is an English estate in the traditional manner – a blend of open lawns and enclosed rose gardens, mature native trees and exotic species from overseas, formal terraces and informal shrubs. There is a contrast between the overt cultivation of the garden, and the more subtle, less obvious management and maintenance of the park and the wider estate to create an appealing yet practical complete landscape.

The estate was bought by successive owners because it was beautiful – but by the beginning of the 20th century, it was probably too small to run as a viable business concern, and its maintenance was only possible because of Mrs Greville's considerable personal fortune. Her passion for the property is undeniable, but her involvement in the garden and grounds was one of consolidation and improvement, rather than radical change. The soil is actually thin, free-draining and limy with a chalk substratum, so not especially suited to luxuriant planting, but Mrs Greville created one of the great Edwardian gardens by persistence, expenditure and expertise on the part of her fifteen gardening staff.

Right The Long Herbaceous Border in summer, looking east towards the house

Below Mrs Greville with a Sikh guest in the Rose Garden

The planting nowadays is not exactly as it would have been in Mrs Greville's time, as her use of Polesden was seasonal. She visited at weekends, hosting large house-parties during Ascot week in June, and over Christmas and the New Year. So the original planting was designed to show the house at its best when she was in residence, and to support her households with produce and flowers. The planting scheme has since been amended to provide visitors with year-long interest.

Mrs Greville's initial plans were ambitious: in 1907 she commissioned a grandiose scheme from landscape architects Durrand, Murray and Seddon, which would have created a complex series of terraces on the south side of the house, with steps leading down to semi-circles of Italian cypresses and Moorish pergolas, with French parterres, terraces and walls. But the sudden death of Captain Greville in 1908 put paid to her enthusiasm, and later she commissioned a more conventional layout – a sequence of linked gardens enclosed by walls or hedges and filled with roses, peonies, lavender and irises. She put in a rose garden and a rock garden, increased the kitchen garden, and installed a golf course (now used for grazing) and tennis courts, both to the north of the house. Impressive historic statues acted as counterpoints to vistas and views, and each element of the garden was designed as a different 'outdoor room', with its own atmosphere and seasonal interest. Mrs Greville's very English garden, with its abundant and colourful bedding plants, was carefully created to appeal to her aristocratic guests, many of them from overseas.

As well as providing opportunities for leisure and pleasure, the gardens were used to provide cut flowers for the house, and fruit and vegetables for the table, especially when Mrs Greville was in residence between May and January. The heated glasshouses, fuelled by 30–40 tons of coke a year, coddled orchids and exotic fruit, and forced peas, beans, potatoes and strawberries in large pots for early crops. Seakale, endive and other exotic delicacies were also raised for the table, and up to 2000 annuals were propagated every year to fill the spectacular flowerbeds. The orchards provided apples and walnuts, and during the Second World War, the Herbaceous Border and the Croquet Lawn were turned over to growing vegetables.

Below The Lavender Walk at the eastern end of the Rose Garden

21

'Won't you come into the garden? I would like my roses to see you.'

Sheridan, to a beautiful female guest at Polesden Lacey

Above The Entrance Front
Right The Rose Garden
Below The Pets' Cemetery

TOUR OF THE GARDEN

The Entrance Front

Outside the main entrance to the house, a ring of Golden English Yew bushes surrounds the forecourt, and a 15th-century Venetian well-head provides a focal point to this frontage, replacing a sundial that stood there in Mrs Greville's time.

The South Lawn

The south front consists of a magnificent portico and lawned terrace, with a pair of limestone griffins and four 18th-century English limestone urns on plinths.

Mrs Greville often asked her royal guests to plant a specimen tree commemorating their visit at the western end of the great lawn that sweeps down from the south front of the house. Unfortunately, all the 'royal' trees were lost during the Great Storm of 1987, though the Atlas Mountain Cedar planted by the Queen Mother in 1977 on the east side of the house has survived, as it was better protected from the force of the gale. Purple thyme grows amongst the grass of the South Lawn, giving off a resonant and attractive smell to visitors.

The Pets' Cemetery

An unusual feature of the garden is the Pets' Cemetery, where Mrs Greville had interred the remains of her beloved pets, with simple, small-scale tombstones, each inscribed with heartfelt dedications.

In a small enclosure, surrounded by yew hedges on three sides, is Mrs Greville's own grave. At the rear of this enclosure are four statuettes of the Four Seasons in terracotta. Spring bears a posy of early flowers, while a circlet of ivy adorns the head of Winter.

The Rose Garden

To the west of the house, a former walled kitchen garden was transformed in Mrs Greville's time into a rose garden. The entrance is flanked by a pair of stone griffins, and at the meeting point of the four large rectangular beds is a 14th-century well-head from the Palazzo Morosini-Sagredo in Venice. Four sculptures of the Seasons, carved from English limestone, flank the north wall.

The planting is mostly early 20th-century in style, with softly pastel roses. The pergolas

bear Edwardian rambling roses; the borders combine shrub roses, geraniums and fuchsias with climbing roses; and dwarf hedges of lavender and box edge the paths.

The Lavender and Iris Gardens
West of the Rose Garden lies a smaller garden with parallel borders of peonies, which were predominantly grown to provide cut flowers for the house.

The adjoining Lavender Garden is filled with many varieties of the plant, which give off an intoxicating aroma in July, ideally enjoyed from one of the many stone seats. The centrepiece is a copy of the famous Greek statue known as the *Discobolos* (Discus Thrower).

The Iris Garden is dedicated to historic varieties of this elegant plant.

The Winter Garden
The Winter Garden has three unusual Iron Trees from Northern Iran, which flower in February. A wide collection of winter aconites, snowdrops and crocus, with other bulbs and shrubs, provides winter and early spring display. Beyond is a picturesque wooden bridge with a thatched roof, which spans a deep service road, created in 1861 to allow estate workers and their vehicles access to the estate without being seen.

The Herbaceous Border
A spectacular 450-foot long border of herbaceous plants flowers every summer, though the site suits drought-tolerant and resistant plants as the soil is poor and watering is difficult. Circular *clairvoyées* (openings) in the wall give tantalising glimpses of the Iris and Lavender Gardens beyond.

The Long Walk
Sheridan's main contribution to the estate was the creation of the Long Walk, a dramatic landscape feature. It was first laid out along the valley in 1761, and was extended by Sheridan in 1816 to a length of 397 metres. Mrs Greville had a yew hedge planted above the ha-ha, which marked the boundary of the garden. Parallel to the Long Walk is the Nun's Walk, lined with beech trees, yews and hollies.

The Croquet Lawn
The Croquet Lawn boasts a lead statue of Diana, the Roman goddess of hunting, copied from an ancient marble group now in the Musée du Louvre in Paris. Cedars of Lebanon were planted on the outer edges of the Croquet Lawn in the 1960s.

Above Statue of Diana at the western end of the Croquet Lawn

Caring for the statues

Conserving Polesden's important statues is a constant challenge: a team of dedicated volunteers – known colloquially as 'the scrubbers' – keeps the statues clean and monitors their condition. Conservation measures are occasionally needed to remedy damage.

THE ESTATE

Driving up to Polesden, after passing under the archway (installed by the National Trust, to a design by Sir Hugh Casson), visitors get hints of the glorious parkland ahead.

There are a number of excellent landscape walks, and the park is a constantly evolving vista of avenues of mature beech trees and lime trees, interspersed with glimpses of the house and the panorama beyond. Sweet and Spanish Chestnuts also grow in the approach to the house. Rhododendrons and conifers benefit from the acid soil around the recently reinstated crab-apple orchard, and there are impressive specimens of Californian Redwood, Wellingtonia, Douglas Fir and Spruce.

The plantations and woodlands were carefully tended as game preserves, and Mrs Greville hosted frequent shooting parties – the unique geography of the site, with the deep valley to the south, lent itself admirably to the shooting of partridge and pheasant.

Above Ranmore Common in autumn. It lies on the southern edge of the Polesden Lacey estate

Below Chauffeurs and mechanics with Mrs Greville's fleet of cars in the Stable Yard

The farms

There are two farms on the Polesden Lacey estate: Goldstone Farm has been tenanted by the same family since 1915, and is grazed by an Ayrshire milking herd. Home Farm (also known as Polesden Farm) is mainly grass, and currently let out for cattle and sheep grazing to a local butcher, whose family business dates back to the 18th century. In Mrs Greville's day, herds of cattle and flocks of sheep – and even prize-winning turkeys – were reared at Polesden, and it was self-sufficient in most produce. Flowers, vegetables, milk, butter and fruit were sent up to London daily, when Mrs Greville was in residence in her Mayfair house.

Working for Mrs Greville

Naturally, maintaining the estate in such style required a great many dedicated staff – up to 70, and their dependents, were accommodated on site. Female domestic staff tended to live in the upper storeys of the house itself, while male staff with families would be allocated housing on the estate – the former Head Gardener's cottage is now a Holiday Cottage. Although they worked longer hours than nowadays – a 52-hour week, from 6am to 6pm, with meal breaks – the gardeners were much in demand to act as caddies on the golf course, a welcome opportunity for them to acquire generous tips.